Canoeman Joe

Robin Radcliffe

illustrated by
Consie Powell

For my own Nora who loves to help her dad in the canoe shop.
- R.R.

For Jeanne
    - C.B.P.

The creation of *Canoeman Joe* has been a collaboration between author and illustrator from early on, and has benefited from contributions from many friends of Joe. We thank the Seliga family for generous support of our effort to bring Joe to a new generation of kids. Joe and Nora's daughters, JoAnn and Nancy, graciously shared family photos, anecdotes and historical details that enriched the story. Bruce Casselton, Tim Eaton and Jerry Stelmok shared insights into the Seliga family's Morris canoes. Camp Widjiwagan warmly welcomed our research into Joe's life and the Widji Seliga canoe legacy. Joe Smith's and Jeanne Bourquin's reminiscences helped bring Joe's character to life, and Jeanne's reflections on helping Joe on the morning of the fire were invaluable. Anne Swenson provided fire photos from the archives of the Ely Echo, and Pam Brunfelt, who now lives at the corner of 3rd and Pattison, welcomed us to snoop the premises. Numerous photos in *Wooden Canoe* (the Journal of the Wooden Canoe Heritage Association) provided excellent reference. *The Art of the Canoe with Joe Seliga* by Jerry Stelmok and Deborah Sussex has been an exceptional resource. Special thanks to our paddling partners, Julia and Nora (for Robin) and Rog (for Consie) who keep our respective canoes true and straight.

This book was made possible in part by a grant from the Donald G. Gardner Humanities Trust of Ely, Minnesota.

The illustrations were created with ink, scratchboard, colored pencils, and watercolor.

10 9 8 7 6 5 4 3 2 1

Green Writers Press is a Vermont-based publisher whose mission is to spread a message of hope and renewal through the words and images we publish. Throughout, we will adhere to our commitment to preserving and protecting the natural resources of the earth. To that end, a percentage of our proceeds will be donated to environmental activist groups and the Nora and Joe Seliga Wood Canoe Fund at Camp Widjiwagan. Green Writers Press gratefully acknowledges support from individual donors, friends, and readers to help support the environment and our publishing initiative. Green Place Books curates books that tell literary and compelling stories with a focus on writing about place—these books are more personal stories, memoir, and biographies.

green
writers
press

GREEN
PLACE
BOOKS

Giving Voice to Writers & Artists Who Will Make the World a Better Place
Green Writers Press | Brattleboro, Vermont
greenwriterspress.com

ISBN: 978-1732854000

Printed on paper with pulp that comes from managed forests that guarantee responsible environmental, social, and economic practices by Printopya.

In a land of water and stone, where rugged miners in candlestick hats filled railcars with Minnesota ore, there lived a boy who loved canoes and wood more than trains and steel.

Other boys listened for the chugs and whistles of the Duluth and Iron Range Railroad, but Joe Seliga listened for the moans and rumbles of lake ice breaking. That meant springtime, and springtime was canoetime in Ely.

"Canoetime!" shouted Joe the day the ice went out. That was the day his father pulled workman sleeves over a white shirt and led Joe to the boathouse on Shagawa Lake. Joe dressed up too, in grey overalls and his favorite green jacket. The pungent aroma of northern white cedar tickled Joe's nose.

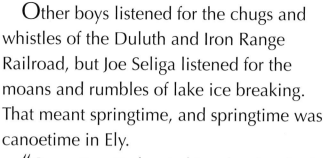

Together they lifted the canoes from their winter beds onto the workshop cradle. Each canoe had been made of wood and canvas by tailored gentlemen from the Morris Canoe Factory in faraway Veazie, Maine. Joe liked the little Morris, the one with soft seats stuffed full of horsehair, most of all.

Joe and his father opened a can of marine paint and filled last summer's scratches with green enamel. Once the hulls were dry, they slid them one by one into the waters of Shagawa Lake. Joe's father paddled while Joe crept from bow to stern probing for dribbles of water.

"No leaks." Joe called to the rest of the family. "Canoetime!"

All spring, Joe and his brothers and sisters paddled the Morrises with their father into Basswood Lake to fish for trout. In the summer, they skirted Fall Lake to fill pails full of berries, and come autumn they hopscotched along the North Arm of Burntside Lake to hunt for grouse. Every Sunday, the Seligas filled the big Morris with biscuits and meat pies for a picnic on the shore of Shagawa Lake. After each journey, the canoes were wiped dry and hung with care in the boathouse.

One day, Joe's father found the boathouse door ajar. The rack where the big Morris rested when not in the water was empty. For many months, Joe searched the lakes, boathouses and backyards around Ely. Joe's father put up a sign at the iron mine, and Joe painted the big Morris onto discarded grain sacks and hung them in the town shops.

LOST CANOE

Joe squeezed between his brothers and sisters around the breakfast table to hear the news.

"Oh, this is good," Joe's father pronounced. "The big Morris has been found up on White Iron Lake!"

When Joe saw that the thief had disguised the boat under a layer of house paint, he made up his mind to repair it. Each day after school, Joe scraped away at the stubborn paint. When he got to the bow and stern, he had to shimmy on his belly to reach splayed stems and tapered cant ribs where the ugly paint clung like lichen to a Minnesota boulder. But Joe was determined, and soon the canoe shimmered like new.

"You have a way with canoes, Joe," his father said. "Will you care for both of the Morrises?" Joe grinned.

Joe took care of the canoes, and they took care of Joe too. They gave him freedom. By the time Joe finished school, he paddled the little Morris by himself up Moose Lake into the Knife Lake Chain where waterways and portage trails connect Minnesota with Ontario. On rocky shores, he waded knee-deep into the cold lake water to land the canoe without scratching the paint or piercing the canvas.

The canoe gave back by splitting wind-tossed waves to keep Joe and his canvas packs dry. And the canoe sheltered him in summer rainstorms. Afterwards, Joe dried the canoe in the warm sunshine before tipping it onto a bed of pine needles beside his canvas tent.

When Joe turned twenty, he met Nora. Nora loved the water and woods as much as Joe did. On weekends, Joe and Nora lashed the little Morris to the high fenders of Joe's father's Model T and bumped north along the Echo Trail to paddle across Burntside Lake and portage into Slim and Hegman. Joe had not yet turned twenty-one when he married Nora. The couple settled into a simple room above the Seliga family home.

Like his father and grandfather before him, Joe got a job in the iron mines. He started as a bullwhacker, coupling the rail cars together. And when he was promoted to skip, he took great care in raising and lowering the cage that carried the miners and ore. Times were tough, so in between posts at the mine, Joe took any odd job that turned up. The town veterinarian hired him to test dairy cows to make sure their milk was safe to drink. He laid sidewalks along Ely streets, and painted houses for three dollars a day. In every spare moment, Joe and Nora paddled the little Morris. Joe and Nora's best days were canoe days.

Joe's worst day came on the Nina Moose River, when he and his father headed out for trout and walleye. With spring waters running high, Joe carried the packs along the flooded portage trail that skirted the Nina Moose while his father cautiously navigated the empty canoe through the fast water.

All of a sudden, Joe heard the unmistakable sound of splintering wood. He ran to the river's edge to find his father pulling himself from the icy water. The canoe bobbed under a downed tree. His father was unhurt, but the Morris suffered twenty-one cracked ribs. Wet and cold, the two patched the broken canoe. It creaked, and water trickled in, so they took turns bailing with a tin cup: scoop, paddle, scoop, paddle, scoop, paddle. At last, they made it to the landing on the Echo Trail.

Big

All summer long, Joe puzzled over the big Morris.

There were no canoe factories nearby, nor wooden boat schools, so Joe would have to figure out how to fix the canoe himself. He put a crooked handle on his hammer to nail in tight spots, and made a clinching iron to bend the canoe tacks.

Joe then experimented with bending ribs. Nora boiled water while Joe laid narrow planks of cedar inside the spare tire tube from the Model T. They tied both ends and added steam. The rubber contraption ballooned up like a giant sausage and heated the wood. Nora laughed at their invention. Joe chuckled too, though he was happy that the canoe builders from Veazie weren't there to see it. Joe pulled a hot rib from the balloon and bent it easily into the curves of the canoe.

Next, Joe pounded tacks while Nora stooped over the canoe to hold the clinching iron up against each new rib. Every time Joe hammered a brass tack through the hull, Nora's heavy iron bent it back over into the soft cedar, clinching it in place.

Afterwards, Joe and Nora admired the orderly dimples.

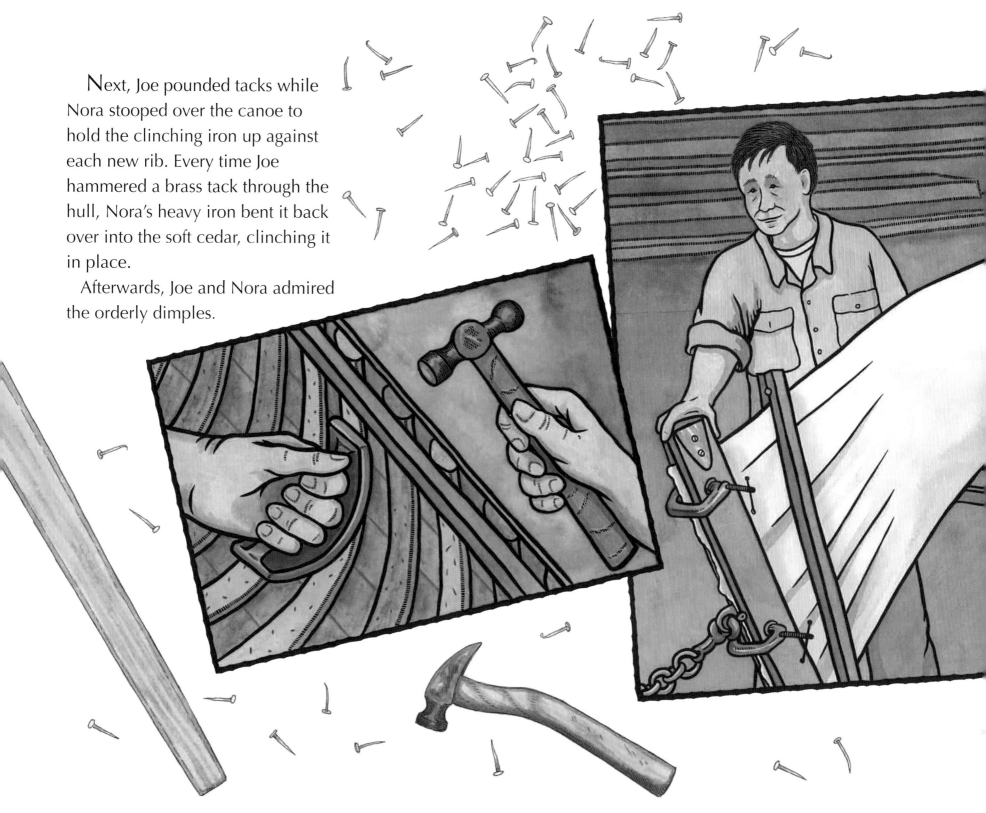

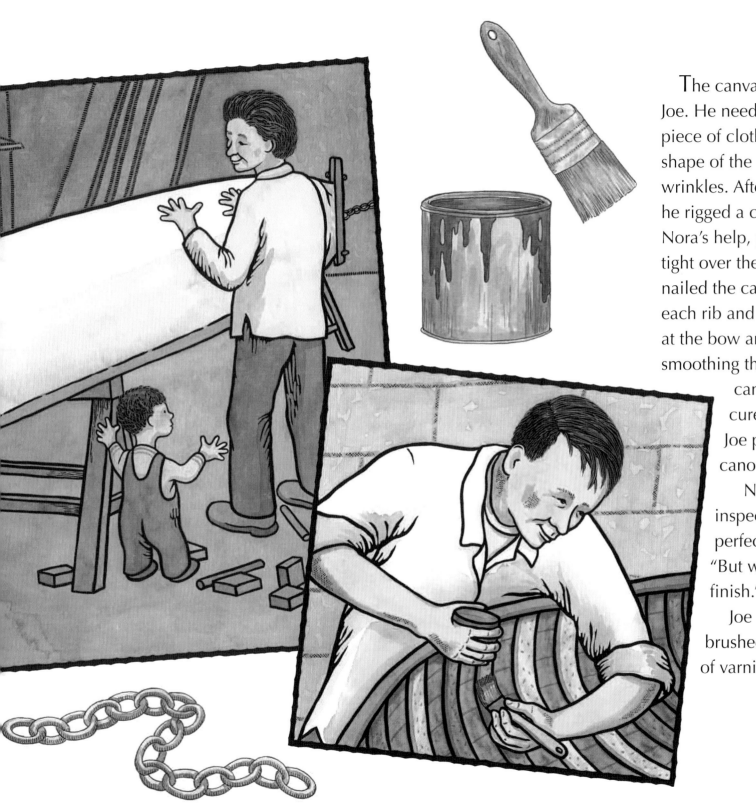

The canvas shell flummoxed Joe. He needed to wrap a flat piece of cloth around the curving shape of the hull without any wrinkles. After much deliberating, he rigged a contraption, and with Nora's help, pulled a canvas sheet tight over the boat's bottom. Joe nailed the canvas to the end of each rib and to wooden stems at the bow and stern before smoothing thick filler into the canvas and leaving it to cure. Three weeks later, Joe painted the hull. The canoe gleamed.

Nora was the canoe inspector. "Your paint is perfect," Nora announced. "But we need a smoother finish."

Joe sanded the hull and brushed on five more coats of varnish until Nora smiled.

Neighbors came to see the restored Morris. They marveled at its beauty, and then began to bring their own boats for Joe to mend.

The day Joe got an order for a new canoe, he fretted. He had never made a canoe, only fixed them. Joe was overwhelmed, but he forged ahead anyway. With an idea in his head, Joe measured the little Morris twice before turning the canoe upside down and covering it with butcher paper. Then he cut a narrow channel in the wide stems and inserted new wooden pieces that stretched the canoe to sixteen feet. Now Joe could use the Morris as a building form. Joe bent hot cedar ribs around its middle, nailing each rib to gunwales lashed beneath.

One by one, Joe fitted planks over the wooden skeleton until the hull was complete. Then, with great care, he signed his name onto a wide plank and blew the ink dry. Joe already knew how to stretch canvas and apply paint and varnish. He added seats, a center thwart, and wooden decks in the shape of a heart. Then he pasted a decal on the bow of the canoe. It read, "Joseph T. Seliga & Son."

Joe had made his first canoe.

Manufactured By
JOS. T. SELIGA & SON
345 E. White St.
Ely, Minnesota

Joe and Nora took their second canoe order from Camp Widjiwagan up the Echo Trail. Then other northwoods camps ordered canoes too: the Sommers Wilderness Canoe Base up on Moose Lake and Camp Menogyn on the Gunflint. Year by year, more and more campers fell in love with Joe's handmade canoes. They learned to land their wooden Seligas without scratching the paint, and to dry them in the warm sunshine before tipping them onto a bed of pine needles.

MFG. BY J.T. SELIGA & SON
THIS IS A GENUINE—
SEL CRAFT
Ely, Minnesota

Joe's canoe building grew with his family. In time, two daughters joined in the Seliga tradition of paddles and picnics around Ely. JoAnn and Nancy helped Nora bake blueberry muffins for the many visitors that came to see Joe, while their older brother Richard helped Joe in the shop.

Over the next fifty-six years, Joe built more than five hundred wood and canvas canoes to carry kids, fishermen, and wilderness guides on journeys into the Boundary Waters Canoe Area and across the border into Quetico Provincial Park. Campers and counselors ordered wooden canoes of their own, and journeyed north on regular visits to see Joe and Nora.

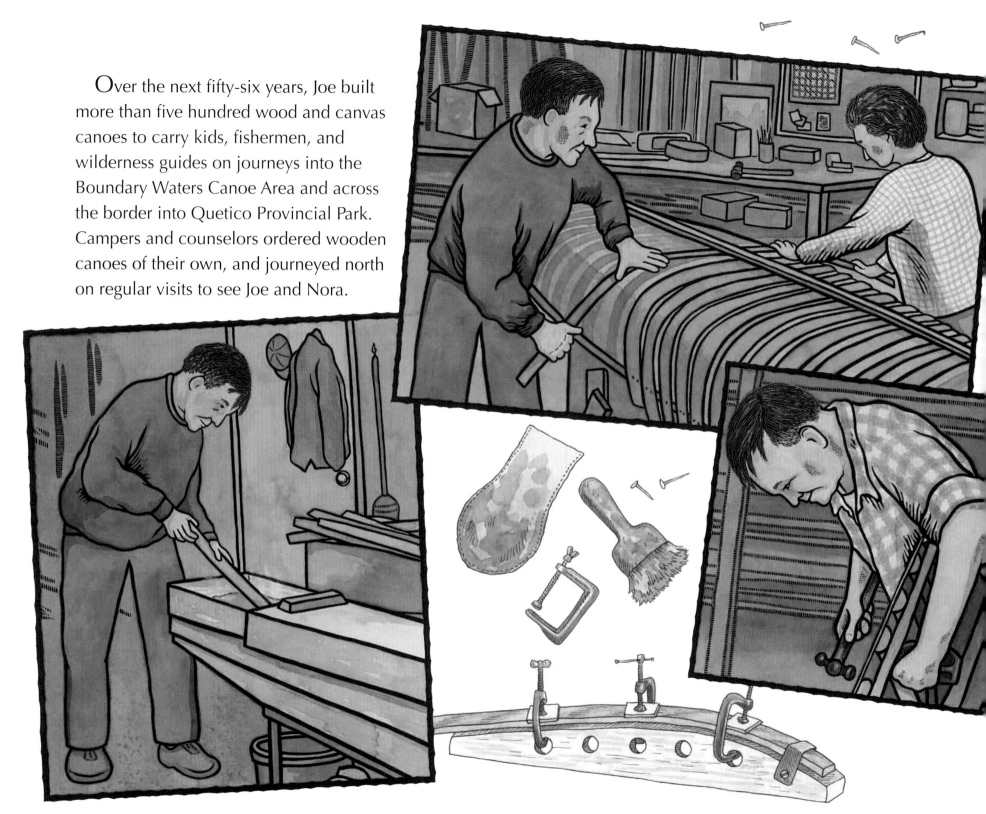

"Remember Number 390?" a Widjiwagan guide asked, smiling. "She was blue!" remembered Joe without opening his builder's notebook. "We made 390 extra deep with a shoe keel for those voyageur trips up Rainy River."

On a frigid morning in February, weeks away from Joe's eighty-third birthday, Nora and Joe shared an early breakfast. Joe washed the dishes before lighting a fire in the shop stove. The cinder block shop was so cold that Joe hurried back inside to sip a second cup of coffee. Nora was the first to see white smoke blowing past the kitchen window.

"Fire!"

Joe raced to the shop. Smoke curled from under the door. When Joe opened it, a blast of heat and dark smells toppled him backwards.

Joe picked himself up and waved down a passing neighbor to call the Ely firehouse. Friends and kin raced up Pattison Street and down East Third to fight the blaze and help Joe pull smoldering planks from the shop. From high in the rafters, a fireman passed down the canoes one by one into the snow. In his matter-of-fact way, Joe gave out directions with a friendly nod and gleam.

The wooden handles had burned off Joe's favorite tools, and his eyebrows were singed, but a smile broke on his face. The little Morris sat steaming in the snow. Its paint was badly blistered and the canvas wrinkled, but it was still there.

Joe comforted the canoe like an old friend. "You're okay, little Morris."

The next morning, Joe and Nora were worn out, but tickled by all who had come to lend a hand. They exchanged a smile on the winding road to Camp Widjiwagan where Joe's salvaged tools, canoes, and materials had been stockpiled.

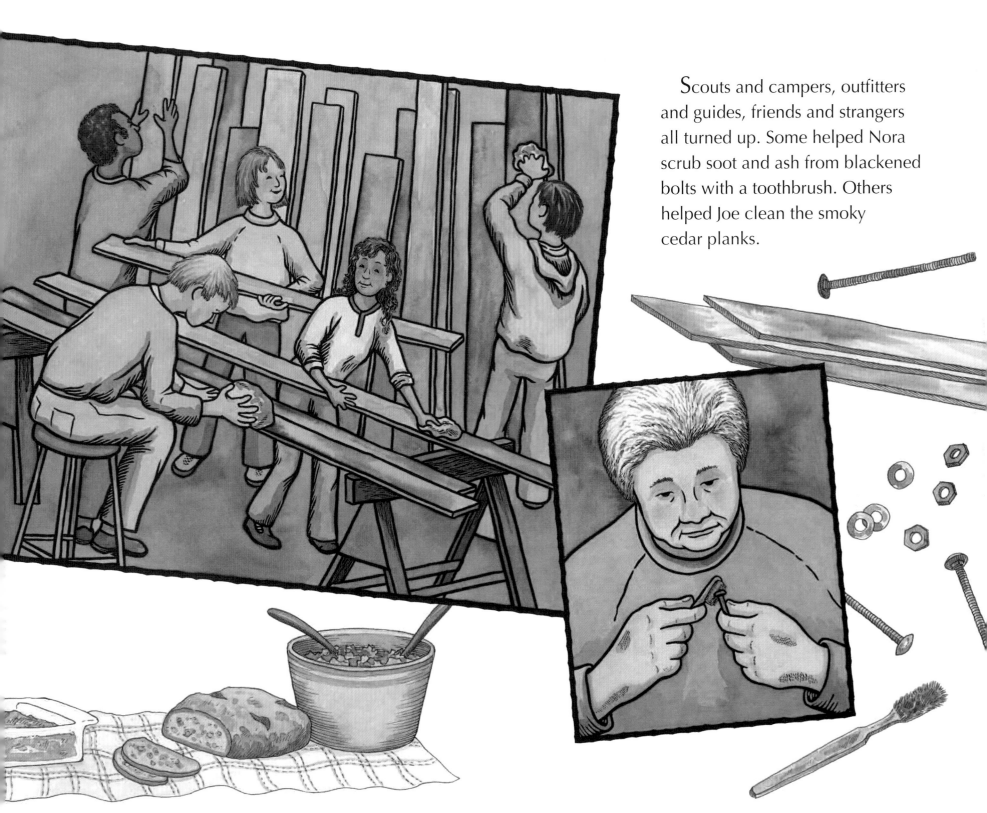

Scouts and campers, outfitters and guides, friends and strangers all turned up. Some helped Nora scrub soot and ash from blackened bolts with a toothbrush. Others helped Joe clean the smoky cedar planks.

Months later, when the weather warmed, Joe began the slow job of rebuilding his shop. Until it was ready, Joe repaired camp canoes at Widjiwagan. And Joe was there on the last day of the Widjiwagan canoe camping season to hear stories of the summer's canoe adventures paddling wooden Seligas into faraway lakes and down wild rivers.

After the stories were over, a camper asked, "Will you build more canoes, Joe?"

Joe grinned and led the campers into the Widjiwagan canoe shop. Nora carried a bag of horsehair. Joe carried his crooked hammer, brass tacks poking from one side of his mouth. He was dressed in grey overalls and his tattered green jacket. Canoeman Joe grinned wider than ever. He motioned for the campers to gather around his cherished little Morris.

"She will take care of you," Joe promised. "But first we must care for her."

Under Joe's watchful eye, the campers stuffed the seats with horsehair until they were soft again. The canoeman tacked the edges. Nora watched Joe reach over and caress the canoe.

"This will be your new home," he whispered.

Joe Seliga faced each day with a wholehearted smile, his good nature belying the difficult work he shouldered as both a boy and a man. Joe was born in 1911 into a big family where chores around the homestead were a way of life — and adventure abounded in the out-of-doors. Like many Ely natives, Joe toiled in the iron mines and worked a variety of jobs to make ends meet. He did this all while teaching himself the intricate craft of wood and canvas canoe building. Joe built a remarkable 619 canoes over a 67-year period, even after a devastating fire took his shop.

The story of Joe Seliga is also the story of Ely, Minnesota. Joe and his wife, Nora, were much loved by the town where four generations of the Seliga family made their home. Ely was founded as a mining community above the rich iron deposits of the Vermilion Range. The ore mined there was so pure that two pieces of rock could be welded together. The mining families stuck together too. Joe remembered his father hosting secret union meetings in their home with the windows blocked off and the miners arriving in intervals. Joe was sent upstairs, but he listened by lying on the floor next to a heat vent.

Ely was, and still is, at the end of the road in northern Minnesota, and the only way due north from Ely is by canoe, dogsled, or bush plane. This land is a remote wilderness area of interconnected waterways. The Seliga canoe was born at the edge of this wilderness — and there it was meant to be paddled.

It all began in 1948 when Joe made four canoes for Camp Widjiwagan, a summer canoe camp for kids. The following year, the Charles L. Sommers Wilderness Canoe Base needed boats to outfit its canoe guides, and when they visited Joe in his shop and learned that he was planning a seventeen-foot canoe model designed for wilderness paddling, they ordered four boats on the spot. Sommers went on to purchase more than 120 of Joe's canoes, but it was Camp Widjiwagan on the north arm of Burntside Lake that established the longest partnership with Joe, beginning in the 1940s and lasting nearly sixty years.

The Seliga canoe is simple and elegant in its form, and impeccable in its workmanship. While retaining the strong influence of canoe-maker

B.N. Morris and his celebrated canoes of Veazie, Maine, Joe's canoes were built for the remote lake country of Minnesota and Ontario. Joe shortened the length of the standard canoe model by one foot to better maneuver through the timbers of a backcountry portage, and he softened the sharp rise at the sheer line so the boat would not be buffeted by lake winds. Joe also deepened the canoe amidships to hold canvas packs for stalwart fishermen and voyageurs.

Joe visited Camp Widjiwagan each summer to repair the fleet of camp canoes. The kids would work alongside him as he told stories of the northwoods and schooled them in the art of caring for a wood and canvas canoe. The name Widjiwagan comes from the Ojibwa word for "comradeship," and with a core mission of teaching young paddlers the proper use and care of its own fleet of canoes, it was inevitable that the camp became home to the Seliga canoe legacy. The young men and women who guided these trips carried with them Joe's good nature and his ability to lead by example. And the kids gained experience and respect for the boats by making extended canoe camping trips into the Boundary Waters Wilderness and the waterways extending far beyond into Canada.

Joe Smith, the Widjiwagan caretaker and Joe's longtime friend, remembers a camping trip later in Seliga's life with fellow canoe-builders Jerry Stelmok and Jeanne Bourquin. Even at eighty-seven, the canoeman loved to pitch a tent and sleep outdoors. Smith remembers Joe waking in the middle of the night and pulling him from his sleeping bag. "I've been thinking," Joe said. "When I'm gone I would like my form to go to Widjiwagan."

Joe died at the age of ninety-four, still building canoes in his small shop on Pattison Street in Ely. The form, his tools, the steam box, assorted jigs for bending wood, and his handwritten records from seven decades of canoe-making are at Camp Widjiwagan, being cared for by a new generation of Minnesotans. Today, Widjiwagan campers still learn the heritage of the wood and canvas canoe; they paddle, portage, load and unload, make small and large repairs, and even build new wooden canoes from scratch in the time-honored Seliga tradition.